The Unstuck Playbook

Five Simple Steps to Live the Life You Want Now

Blossom Birch

This book is dedicated to my parents for their sacrifice, discipline and love that propelled me to where I am today.

To my children, my love personified. You have everything in you to continue to thrive.

To my Abba, where would I be without you? You are my everything and I thank you!

Contents

Foreword

There comes a time in the life of each and every one of us when the path ahead becomes blurred.

Now more than ever, we are faced with global uncertainty in many areas. On an individual level, sometimes it is the uncertainty of which path to take. Other times it is simply the demands of our day-to-day lives that drain the energy we need to define our next steps.

Perhaps it is not the defining of the next step but rather the consistent execution required to bring our dreams into reality. And let's not forget the unforeseen challenges that leave us physically drained, exhausted, and emotionally bankrupt.

If we can be honest with ourselves, sometimes the choices we make to create happy times have their own heavy consequences. Regardless of where you are or how you got there, feeling stuck is a sentiment everyone can relate to.

To make matters worse, it is very easy to feel stuck when defeat has been living with you, and success seems to come for an occasional visit. I can relate. However, I realized a long time ago that no one was coming to my rescue. If change was going to come, it had to start with me.

The second thing I realized was this: How I choose to respond during challenging times will either help me or hurt me. I began to view challenges as opportunities to learn and grow.

Perspective is everything.

Your beliefs are the fuel that will drive your life.

Right now, everyone is faced with some level of uncertainty. The COVID 19 pandemic hopefully taught us how unpredictable life is. It was difficult for most people to be hopeful, during this time as the focus quickly shifted to the negative news. More negative news was reported despite the heroism of the brave front-line workers who were battling and winning during this very devastating period. Life as we knew it changed suddenly, and everyone felt stuck. We must realize there are some things we have no control over, but we must do all we can to stay positive and remain focused.

Your focus will be your reality.

Although these are unusually demanding times, use them as an opportunity to get ahead. Don't let life's troubles hold you back from your dreams. You have the power to overcome anything. Fight to become who you envision yourself to be! The benefit will far exceed the effort you put in.

I used to live not defeated but very stagnant, waiting for my fate to change. But I've learned not to waste time anymore. The stagnation time in my life was simply based on what I believed. It has been quite a few years now, and I have often been asked, "How do you do it?" or, "How do you do it all and have the energy to keep going and smiling?"

People who know me well have asked how I can still be happy with all that I have gone through. I will most certainly answer these questions for you later, but let me take a moment to introduce myself and give you a glimpse into what my daily schedule used to be so you can see, if I can make it, so can you.

Who is Blossom Birch? I am a carrier of God's grace and a student of all that is within my purpose. I am humble and submissive, and I know my worth. I am an ambivert, introverted by default, but equally extroverted because I never let the mission fail. I am a silent gladiator. I am also a happy mother of two beautiful and amazing girls. Between work, school and sports, my girls and I have hectic schedules.

I have no family or support system where I live, and I usually work ten to twelve hours six days a week, with an additional three hours of commuting time each day. And, until midway through writing this book, I was taking care of my aging mother (RIP Mom). You'll hear more about that later. I also took care of my father for ten years before he transitioned.

When you are the caregiver of your parents and raising young children at the same time, there is very little time for yourself. There were days I just wanted to escape from it all, but like many of you, I did my best to keep going.

I know how it feels to be stuck and to be unsure of which direction to take. Life pulls you through hills and valleys. How you move forward will establish how you face the next challenge. Your mindset and actions will determine your success, so your next steps are critical. Later, I will dive into some best practices for making progress.

Sometimes, I wonder if the challenges choose me or if I choose them.

Many of us have faced very trying circumstances. Sometimes, it is difficult to move forward, so you resign yourself to the routine you know. Be aware this may be the foundation for stagnation.

Regardless of how the challenge comes about, I have learned to determine my end from the beginning. This is why I am so excited to walk you through a very simple process I call my unstuck playbook. These steps have helped me and many others tremendously, and they will most certainly help you to live the life you want.

You may feel stagnant. Work and life are maybe mundane, and you are tired of being tired. Perhaps you have tried to start a business or to go back to school while deciding on a career change. Maybe you want to commit to exercising more and eating better, but life gets in the way of your progress.

You may have had some success, but the passion and energy you had may have plateaued in some areas of your life. Perhaps you have experienced a loss or have health concerns. Possibly, you may be feeling stuck in a job and want better, but you need your daily bread and are not sure how to move on.

Perhaps 'you're overwhelmed with the demands of life, family, and work. Maybe you've lost someone or you are a caregiver to a family member and it is draining your energy. Maybe you have had an unforeseen financial setback.

Perhaps you're not in the relationship you desire. Maybe you're not connecting well with your significant other. Perhaps you are single and concerned about the options you have entertained or whether you will be in the relationship you desire. To add to your turmoil, the reality of your day-to-day routine does not help your progress because, the truth is, you are carrying a lot of weight while trying to stay afloat.

Let Me Assure You of Two Things:

1. You are not alone.
2. This book will guide you through five simple steps to create a success plan and take one small step towards progress. Then, you can repeat what works and adjust when the waves come in.

Chapter 1

Establish Clarity

"Clarity is the invisible roadmap that guides our thoughts and actions."

— Blossom Birch

Before we move on, let me clarify one critical area for you. You might think you need to make massive changes in order to achieve the life you want now. This is not true at all! Let me explain why. Every great endeavor begins with one small step. That's it, take one small step and be consistent daily, weekly or as often as possible. We tend to think that we need to do so much at once to achieve what we want. Thinking this way will overwhelm you very quickly, and we know what happens after that.

Steven Kotlier, the author of The Rise of Superman, describes how an insane feat by an athlete, a feat that appears to be impossible, actually started with one small step. He studied athletes who performed in extreme sports, and he also studied Olympians. He found out that each of them started the same way. They were regular people, like you and me, many with no coach in the beginning. They all began with one practice session and failed many times, but they kept going. Over time, they mastered a skill far beyond anything they dared to dream. This is because repetition is the mother of skill.

Repetition is the mother of skill.

Chapter 1

It all starts with taking one small step toward your goal. Now that we understand that achieving the life you want begins with one small step, the means by which you take that step begins with the following two questions:

1. What do you believe?
2. Why do you believe it?

You must take the time to be very clear about these two questions. Your beliefs are critical to how you think. Your thoughts become your words, and your words become your actions. What you envision for your future will directly influence how you live.

What you envision for your future will directly influence how you live.

Regarding your reason, you must understand what is driving you. Why do you want the dream you are after?

1. Is it a certain lifestyle you're after?
2. Is it a better life for your children and your family?
3. Is it freedom from the 9 to 5?

Even if you only have yourself, YOU are enough reason to push for you. Remember, you don't have to have all the answers, but you must have your reason why. To implement these ideas, you MUST write down your belief and your "Why"

As I mentioned, you don't have to have all the answers, energy or resources when you begin. If necessary, drag yourself to take the first small step toward the life you want, and keep taking small consistent steps. Start your morning with a clear mind. Take time out daily to evaluate yourself. Also, give yourself credit for any tiny step you have taken.

Remember, your day will start depending on how you ended the night before. For me, when I wake up, I take a few minutes to clear my mind and pray. I thank God for the opportunity of life and ask for guidance throughout my day. Then I write down one small step I need to take toward my goal, or review what I wrote the night before and add something to be excited about.

Usually, at night, I journal my day and evaluate how I did. Holding yourself accountable this way at the end of every day is the path to achieving the life you want. Your belief is the fuel that will drive your life.

Chapter 2

Eliminate Stagnation

Every Action Starts In Your Mind.

Now that we have clarified the myth of having to take massive action to achieve success, let's get into why we may feel stuck and exactly what we need to do to eliminate stagnation.

The reality of life's journey, as I mentioned earlier, will take you through some days of hills and valleys, and sometimes the speed at which they occur will leave you dizzy. This is expected.

Sometimes, the choices we make leave us with a result we did not expect. Perhaps you have tried everything you can think of, and still do not get the result you are looking for. You get frustrated and tired, and you don't want to try again because you don't want to deal with the pain of failure. This makes you settle where you are and remain in your comfort, or really, your discomfort zone. You're stuck.

This is understandable. No one wants to be frustrated time and time again. However, the truth of the matter is you cannot remain in this state, and you know it deep inside of you. It does not serve you well.

Settling will never bring you joy or fulfillment. As a matter of fact, it is developing the life you do not want to live. To eliminate stagnation, or become unstuck here are the five simple, but very effective steps to live the life you want now:

1. Get rid of negative beliefs.
2. Decide who you want to become.
3. Take action and be relentless.
4. Get help! Please!
5. Prepare for success.

1. Get Rid of Negative Beliefs

- What do you believe about yourself?
- Is it serving you well?

The fact is your belief shapes your outcome. Every action starts in your mind. Every step you take begins with what you believe.

The truth is, if you don't envision yourself as successful now, and if you don't speak positively about yourself, you will not be successful. It is that simple.

If you believe that you may or may not be successful, then you are battling double-mindedness. You question if you can really make it happen. You second guess if you can succeed, and you list all the reasons why you can't, you list all failures you've had, and you replay them in your mind.

The truth is if you don't envision yourself as successful now, and especially if you don't speak positively about yourself, you will not live the life you desire. It is that simple.

The capacity of a fixed mind is POWERFUL! You are simply where you are because of what you believe.

On the flip side, if you believe you can achieve what you desire and will do whatever it takes, then your energy will change, urging you to take the required action. To drive this point deeper, let's say you want to lose some weight, and you set a goal to get to the gym three times a week. You begin strong, but life gets in the way, and you're too tired to exercise. Perhaps you work long hours and can't get up early in the morning, or you're taking care of your family. Perhaps your job is very demanding and leaves you exhausted. Does this sound familiar?

The truth of the matter is, you had that job or circumstance before you decided to lose weight. You did get started trying to lose the weight, but something changed, and you began to tell yourself that it is too difficult.

You will be surprised at what your mind and body can accomplish when you push past the difficulty and stick to your goal. Maybe you can aim at going to the gym once or twice a week, and make up for the other exercise time at home. Whatever you decide, just keep taking one small step daily. I am continuing with the exercise theme to drive home the power of a made-up mind. If you tell yourself, regardless of my heavy schedule, I need to lose weight. I am going to do whatever it takes to make it happen your brain will begin to process what you have said, and your actions will begin to change.

Every single thing we do starts in our mind

Keep in mind that our minds are an accumulation of thoughts, beliefs and influences from our environments. Perhaps growing up, you were told, this is how we are in this family. We are big people. That belief from whatever you were told as a child has stuck with you subconsciously, so losing weight has been difficult.

Now let's go to the extreme and say you heard mostly negative statements growing up and did not have the love and encouragement you needed in your formative years. Perhaps you were bullied so you grew up very timid, and you don't see yourself as someone who can be a high achiever. Maybe you did not have the love needed from both parents as a child and have some resentment or some issues that were buried so deep and never addressed.

It is very understandable if you have not progressed the way you should because you have been so immensely influenced by what you saw and what you heard or the lack thereof. And I am not even addressing the pain or abuse that you may have experienced that crippled your thinking or belief.

Now that you are older and have made some progress and are in a better position than your past, you may have become comfortable with where you are. However, there is a desire inside of you for better. Perhaps you have tried and failed, or you don't know where or how to start.

You feel stuck because you are tired of trying, and don't have the discipline to consistently make progress. Maybe you keep procrastinating and putting off for tomorrow or perhaps have given up on your dreams. You are either not determined enough for your dreams or silently having an affair with fear. Fear will cripple you, and it will trap you in a cave.

Fear will cripple you, and it will trap you in a cave.

I call the cave Adullam. It is a difficult place to be, painful, yes, but you can use the cave time to plan and prepare. In the Bible, Adullam is where David hid from King Saul. During his hiding, David did not cower. No, he used his time in the cave to plan and to train. Other men joined him there, and he became captain of 400 men in that cave.

It is in the cave that David became relentless and the man who could have killed Saul, his enemy, but he chose not to do so out of respect for a King and later he himself became king of Israel. Your time in Adullam, feeling stuck or being in a cave, can be positive or negative. I have developed so much from being in Adullam. Now it's your turn. Go ahead, be David!

Motivate yourself out of stagnation. How? By changing your belief and taking action consistently.

You are hindering your progress when you play negative thoughts from your past in your mind, those thoughts confirm your pain and fears. Fear is a very natural emotion. However, whatever you feed will grow. Why are you choosing to feed your fear? My mother used to say, "Why worry when you can pray?" Fear truly cripples you, so why not try this: Feed your faith!

Faith is the substance of things hoped for and the evidence of things unseen.

— Hebrews 11:1.

I like to say that faith is the currency you use to purchase that which you do not have. If faith is currency, then kick fear in the you know what and feed your faith!

Understand this: Your past does not determine your future. Where you started does not determine where you will end.

Let's take Oprah as an obvious example. She tells how she was an accident child, or what we call a one-night stand. She grew up with her grandmother, no mother or father, and very poor, with no electricity or running water in her home. Today, she is one of the most sought-after people in the world. Her influence changed the nature of the talk show forever. Her show was not just a talk show. It was a movement toward kindness and generosity that has continuously been given to thousands worldwide.

Other talk show hosts followed Oprah's lead. They encouraged paying it forward. They encouraged generosity. Audiences and viewers around the world paid attention and followed the inspiration to be their best selves. Random Acts of Kindness and Pay it Forward caught on with many other talk show hosts and people around the world benefited.

Another example is Tony Robbins; he grew up extremely poor as well, in a broken home, often faced with severe hunger. Today he is proactive in feeding the poor and is a world-renowned life coach. Some of the most influential people in the world seek his time. Tony remembers his childhood of being too poor for a Thanksgiving turkey. Now, his partnership with the Feeding America program feeds millions of Americans who struggle with hunger.... including making sure that they receive Thanksgiving turkeys!

How do you think Oprah Winfrey and Tony Robbins, as examples, made it with all the odds stacked against them? They both will tell you that it started with one small step at a time, and the need to get rid of the negative beliefs.

Begin today by believing that the terrible situation that

happened to you or the negative statements that were told to you do not define who you are.

In addition, if you continuously say "I can do whatever I put my mind to" you will begin to feel and think differently. The power of your words is critical. We live and die by what we say. So, be intentional with your words.

You cannot work hard towards the life you want to live and say something negative about your future every day. What you say comes from your thoughts and beliefs. Listen to this carefully: You can change your belief by what you say. Words are powerful! They are especially powerful when you face adversity. Say This is going to work for my good!

I remember some years back when I built my first Single family home. I was so excited to see the finished product. I got the keys, drove to my new home, and put the keys in the front door. When I opened the door, the ceiling from the second level had leaked so badly that the entire first floor was flooded! I was so disappointed. But I immediately said "This is going to work for my good!" I could not sleep in the house. I contacted the builder, and they came out immediately to assess what had happened. The damage was terrible! However, I kept telling myself that this would work for my good even though I had no idea how it was all going to turn out. I repeated, "It is going to work for my good, so much that my mind believed it, and I was at peace.

In the end, the builder agreed to everything I wanted. I even got additional features that I could not afford when I bought the house. The builder wanted to make sure I was pleased. They wanted to rebuild my trust in their business. It all started with what I kept repeating, and it surely worked for my good. I can give you many more examples, but trust that your words have power.

Try it for yourself: Speak positively before you start your day and all throughout your day. Catch yourself when you start to say something negative, even if it is a reality. Flip your words quickly to say something positive. Make what you say more powerful than what you see!

Keep speaking positively. Do it every day, throughout the day, and watch what happens around you. Your brain will begin to process your energy in a positive way. You will be inspired from the inside, and the outside will have no choice but to follow.

Speaking positively is also one nice way to relieve stress. No matter how difficult life gets, speaking positively will work for your good.

Again, the first step to turning your life around is to eliminate the negative beliefs and speak what you want to see.

In order for you to achieve more, you MUST decide who you want to become.

2. Decide Who You Want to Become

Regardless of where you are in life, there is a desire deep inside of you for more. You may be challenged to define who you want to become, but you know you want more. In order to achieve more, you MUST decide who you want to become or what you want to accomplish.

Your desired state does not have to be perfectly clear or carved in stone. You can always make changes along the way, but you need to decide who you want to become or what you want to do.

If it is not clear to you yet, at the very least, you know what you do not want to become. Also, pay attention to the patterns in your life. What do you do that brings you joy? What can you do over and over and over easily, and it does not drain your energy? Now, what robs you of time even though you may enjoy the moment? Some activities in our lives may be a sweet ride, but the destination may be damaging. Take note of what fuels you and what robs you. See the pattern.

What I am referring to in terms of patterns are the things that you enjoy, that seem natural for you, that you don't mind the energy it takes, and it does not rob you.

Write these patterns down to track whatever they may be. They may be clues to who you will become. Keep in mind that becoming does not have an age limit. Whether you are aged 7 or 70 you can become whatever you consistently focus on. The good news is that you have it in you already. You have massive potential inside of you.

You have massive potential inside of you.

It only needs to be nurtured.

To help you live the life you want, follow these simple steps to bring your vision into reality. Perhaps you may already know who you want to become, but it is a challenge getting there. If so, it is time to do what I call self-inventory. I want to provide you with the clarity you need to articulate where you want to be and to develop a plan to get there.

Ask yourself these questions, write down your answers, and be bluntly honest with yourself.

1. What is the compelling reason behind what you want to achieve? The why.
2. Where are you spending the majority of your time?
3. Who are you surrounded by? Are they serving you well?
4. Who is getting a lot of your attention? Is this robbing you of valuable time?
5. What should you start doing?
6. What should you stop doing?
7. What habits do you have? Are they serving you well?

They might not be life-threatening habits, but they might be time, energy, pleasure, or money-sucking habits that would serve you well to lose.

1. What are you eating? It may be causing you to be sluggish.
2. Are you exercising?
3. Are you having a silent affair with fear?
4. Do you really like who you are? If so, great! If not, why?
5. Do you find yourself repeating the same mistakes?
6. Are you free from the pain and hurt of your past?

Have you forgiven whoever hurt you? If so, great; if not, get help and talk to a professional who is trained to help you identify and unpack the pain so you can live a free and happier life.

If not, holding back forgiveness is keeping you hostage. What will life look like if you are free? Nelson Mandela said, Resentment is like drinking poison and expecting the other person to die.

Are the answers to the above questions in line with who you want to become?

Take the time and do yourself a favor by answering these questions. The answers will help you determine why you are feeling stuck. The questions are intentionally simple, but they will free you to become who you want to be. It is also an excellent plan for making progress.

Now, don't beat yourself up if the answers to some of these questions make you uncomfortable. Life may have been or is challenging, but you can most certainly change the trajectory of the turns and arrive at a beautiful place.

The more consistent you are toward daily execution, the better you will be at making progress.

3. Take Action and Be Relentless

After you have eliminated negative beliefs and established who you want to become or what you want to do, the third step is to take action. As I mentioned, take little steps so you can develop the habit of taking action daily. The more consistent you are toward daily execution, the better you will become at making progress.

Remember, repetition is the mother of skill. Some will tell you to take massive action, and I do agree with that.

It does work. But what if you don't have it in you to do that right now? If you have been feeling stuck and you are now following these steps, I suggest that you take little steps in the beginning to build your momentum so you are not overwhelmed.

Taking small steps toward your goal will also allow you to see some quick progress or recognize quick failures. Many people see failure as a major setback, and they quit, but failure comes to inform you. It is the road you must travel to get to success, so change your perspective.

Also, understand that whatever you fail at, or whatever may not work out immediately, does not mean it will not work out later. You must be determined, focused, and relentless in pursuing your goals. This is the very reason you must be very clear on your "why". Document your "why" it becomes even more real. Dig deep within yourself and affirm why you must make progress. Be hungry for what you are after. If you are truly hungry, you will find a way to eat!

Now, if you are not entirely clear at this point in your life because you are starting out and growing into what you want to do, that's OK. Don't beat yourself up for not having everything well-defined. It will come. Continue to follow these steps toward making progress, and soon, you will be able to identify what you want to do or what you definitely do not want to do.

Remember, execution is everything!

The action that you take now will help you shape the future that you envision.

You may have the best idea in the world and have done what you need to do to eliminate negative beliefs. You have documented what you want to do, but if you do not take action, it will never come to pass.

You can't imagine how many times I heard the word no when pursuing my goals. If I had given up, I would not be where I am today. You see, I am starting over too. After a 17-year marriage, I am learning to navigate life as a single mom. Before, my life was certain (or so I thought). Then, I saw my family structure deteriorate.

One day, I looked down and had to face the truth that the foundation I was standing on was broken. But a tiny voice from my inner core told me that I was going to be okay. My faith anchored me. I started taking little steps. I worked hard to eliminate stagnation, and I became relentless in taking action. And now, I have built a new foundation for my girls and me. I am proud of who I have become. But I am not done.

I am not done because of my "Why." Yes, I push for myself and for my family, but there are many people out there that no one else pays attention to, and I know I can influence them, too. I will leave a positive impact on my children and this world. I will do what God put me on this earth to do. This is what drives me. This is my why.

Life was not designed for us to walk alone.

4. Get Help! Please!

Yes, you can do it alone and succeed, but it may take you longer, and it will be less fun.

Highlight areas within your plan that may be a challenge to accomplish. Get someone who is great in that area to help. If you don't know anyone and can't afford it, pay for professional help.

Sometimes it is not the how to you need to figure out; it is just the who you need to help you get it done.

There are many online tutorials and other resources that are inexpensive. In addition, find someone you truly trust and ask that person to hold you accountable for the process. If you don't have someone, keep moving anyway. It may be a little more difficult, but you need to fight for you.

You need to fight for you.

I know this all too well. In my life, I have not had a mentor or coach or people I could lean on.

I became independent, or I should say on my own, at age 16. I had just finished high school. Yes, I finished at age 16. I had my life all planned out. After graduation, I would go on to college and be done by age 20. After that, I would get a job and complete my master's degree by age 23.

None of it happened that way. Right after I graduated from high school, my parents lost everything they had worked for. Not from anything they did wrong but simply from an economic downturn. Sometimes those in positions of power don't make the best decisions for the masses.

Shortly thereafter, my father grew very ill and could not work. The cost of his medication was astronomical without insurance. Both my mother and I were working, but we could not keep up.

I knew I wanted to do better than where I was, and I just couldn't see a way out.

I had to get two jobs to help keep a roof over our heads and help take care of my dad. I would eat one banana a day and drink a two-liter bottle of water to try not to feel the hunger pains. I was in college and working two jobs with no car. I can laugh now, but it was not funny back then. I could not hang out with friends because my schedule did not allow time for entertainment. My schedule was demanding and looking back it was only by God's grace that I survived.

My daily routine was as follows:

Wake up at 4:30 a.m.

Catch the 5:15 AM bus to get to the metro station and change over to the 70 bus at 6:00 a.m.

Arrive at school at 6:45 a.m. and run to my 7:00 a.m. class. Run to back-to-back classes until 11:45 a.m. Then, I ran to catch the noon bus back to the metro because I had to be at my first job by 1:00 p.m. and work on my feet until 5:30 p.m.

After that, I went to my second job by 6:30 and worked until 10:30 p.m. I took two more buses to get home by 11:45 p.m. or 12 midnight.

Study until 1:00 a.m. with my feet in a bucket of cold water so I Don't fall asleep, and I wake up at 4:30 a.m. the next morning to do it all over again five days a week, and work 12 hours on Saturday for a little extra.

Sunday was the only day I did not work because I had told both of my employers that it goes against my Sabbath day. My mother always told me to hold on to reading my Bible as it would give me strength. I figured I needed all the strength I could get. Therefore, Sunday had to be an off day, even though I desperately needed the money.

This crazy schedule of mine went on for about two years, and I eventually had to quit school. Even though I was doing well in all my classes, with barely enough time for studying, I just physically could not keep up, and I still could not afford tuition.

What Is Your "Why?"

I continued working, but I knew that what I was making was not enough to cover my rent, buy medicine for my father, and pay for college. However, my desire for school never left me. I knew I wanted to do better than where I was. I just could not see a way out.

I was stuck and in a rut. I needed a better job, but I also knew I needed my degree to get a better job. I was only a teenager, probably 18 at the time, and I just could not see my way out, especially taking care of both parents and a sick dad with diabetes and Alzheimer's disease.

My father eventually passed away after about 10 years of being ill. The day he died started out as an ordinary day. Then, his frailty seemed to disappear. He sat up in bed for the first time in months. He asked by name about all his children. He even made a joke about someone coming to marry my mom. I asked him, Daddy, is today different? He nodded his head.

Then, he convinced Mom to take a break. She was exhausted from working long hours and caring for her husband. They were high school sweethearts, did everything together, and married for over forty years. He probably figured she would not be able to watch him pass. They had a conversation right before she left, and she kissed him goodnight as she customarily did. Shortly after my mother left, he and I had a beautiful conversation.

He said something that stuck with me, "Blossom, you're the youngest, but you're the oldest." I didn't quite understand at the time, but I do now. I was comfortable being alone with him as I had prayed and asked God for me to be with him when he passed. We talked for a while and I asked him if it was time and he said yes.

I also asked him if he was afraid, and he said, "Just the fear of the unknown." I told him to go towards the light, and I kissed him goodbye, and he passed.

Just like that, my father was gone. I was numb, but had to now plan a funeral, and take care of my mother and my newborn baby girl, so I had to keep moving.

Life was tough, to say the least, but I knew I had to fight for my mother, baby girl, and for myself now. A few years passed, and I eventually got my undergraduate degree. I went on to get two master's degrees from very highly accredited universities. I raised a family with two girls I am very proud of, and, as of the time of this writing, I'm still caring for my beautiful mommy.

This is why it is critical to establish a "why" even if you do not have all the answers for where you want to be.

Many people work very hard to become successful but never plan to live successfully.

5. Prepare for Success

This is the one area most people overlook. Let me be very straight with you. Success might take you to a place that you cannot handle. Remember this and plan not to fall when you arrive.

Once again, this is why it is critical to understand why. What is driving your need to achieve more? I hope you are dreaming big. Not because big is better, but honestly, you have no idea of your potential and the capacity of your mind. You have no clue of the impact and influence you could have on this world, even if it is just one person you influence. That one person may influence thousands, and it all started with you.

Look at where the world is today. Yes, if you have the money and influence, you could make massive changes worldwide, in your community, or in your own home. But more important than money and influence are heart, courage, and persistence. These are what it takes to make the biggest changes of all!

Now, let's get back to our focus for this area. Planning for success is the best gift you can give yourself in this process. Preparing for success will help you to stay successful once you get there.

- Ask yourself, "If I have everything I want, who will I become?"
- Picture yourself at that stage in life.
- What does life look like? What do you have?
- Who is around you? Who can you trust?
- Who have you become?
- Do you like who you are?
- And are you truly happy?

Take the time, find a quiet place, and quiet your mind. Relax and listen for a few minutes.

You must understand your "why."

Now see yourself for who you want to be. Write down how you plan to remain successful. This is critical! Again, it does not have to be extensive but stick to your plan of what you need to put in place in order to remain successful.

Hire a professional for all of your life plans. Get with someone you trust. Find a highly recommended fiduciary and even get a life coach, to help you implement your plan.

There are two financial freedom books I'll recommend: 1. *Money Master the Game* and 2. *Unshakable* by Tony Robbins. Get them today.

Understand that success is not only about money. Wealth is way more than money. Wealth begins with staying true to yourself and maintaining your integrity. What will you say 'no' to in order to keep your integrity intact?

I was sitting in the laundromat not far from. A few years ago, I was sitting in a laundromat near a woman and her son. The little boy could not have been more than four or five years old. He asked his mom for money to get him some candy and she said no. The little boy asked his mom, "Mom, are we poor?" His mom raised her eyes and gently took her son's hand and said, "You have two hands, two eyes, and two feet; you are rich! The little boy looked at his mom and smiled as if he understood the depth of what she said.

I was so moved I wanted to open my purse and give the little boy everything I had, but I immediately realized I could not diminish what his mother had so powerfully done. Those words she spoke to her son during his formative years will shape his future forever.

I say the same to you now; You are here, you have the gift of life. You are already rich!

Act like it! Some people whose wealth is only financial are miserable. Know this also, the journey with money and fame may take you on a sweet ride, but ' don't get seduced by the glitz and the glamor. Make sure the destination is worthy of you.

You may not be all you want to be now, but you have VALUE!

You are worth way more than you give yourself credit for. Your values should not change because you have more money.

Lastly, make wise decisions starting from today. You have often heard that we live and die by the choices we make. It is very true. I tell my girls to make decisions today that will benefit their tomorrow. The decisions you make may not always be popular, but know yourself; understand your weaknesses, and move away from what will make you fall even if it feels good. Make good decisions even when no one is watching.

Making wise decisions when planning for success will help you with the following:

- Solidify your values
- Reinforce your "why"
- Shape your path toward a more successful life
- Influence many along the way.
- Give you peace and build your self-worth before you make your millions.

Planning for success this way is absolutely necessary if you want to remain successful. And when the big payday comes, you will remain firmly rooted in who you are because you have been living successfully all along?

Chapter 3

Don't Quit

You Must Fight For What You Want.
Your Effort Must Equal Your Expectations.

The above statements are true. You must fight for what you want, and your effort must match your expectations. Never quit, no matter how difficult life gets. All of this is true, and I mean it from my heart.

However, what do you do when life unexpectedly turns left and veers completely out of control? Saying, don't quit is more easily said than done when the pain in your day-to-day life cripples your zeal, dims the brightness in your eyes, steals your smile, and immobilizes your thoughts. Let me tell you what happened as I was writing this book.

In August 2021, we were finally able to take a family vacation after being in lockdown mode for almost two years due to the pandemic. My mom couldn't go on the trip because she and my stepdad had a few doctor appointments scheduled. After we got back from vacation, I flew out to take Mom to one more doctor's appointment. The plan was to bring her and my stepdad back to spend Thanksgiving and Christmas with us.

The day before her appointment, my mom had eaten some food that my older brother bought for her, which did not sit well with her, and she threw up most of the night. In the morning, her doctor told her that she had a bowel obstruction and that he wanted to hospitalize her overnight for observation.

Of course, I stayed with her through the night. The tests confirmed that she needed bowel obstruction surgery. The doctor then suggested that during surgery, he would take some tissue from her lungs to get to the bottom of her persistent cough.

I called home to tell the girls that I would be staying with Grandma for about three days and then would bring her home with me. Those three days turned into twenty-seven days. You see, Mom was suddenly diagnosed with stage IV lung cancer.

How could that be? She had always been healthy and had just received a clean bill of health from her complete physical a few months back. She was active;

she never drank, and never smoked. The news left me frozen. I was truly stuck! Part of me wanted to escape from it all, but I knew I had to be strong for my mother and my daughters.

And this is where I must take a sidebar and bring you into the family theatrics that made this unbearable scenario in my life even worse. As previously mentioned, what do you do when life takes a left, and then takes an even sharper left? We all know that family is a great blessing, but sometimes, it is also a source of struggle, a tug of war, a pool of insults, and hurt feelings. I include it here in the Don't Quit section of the book to show you that you can get unstuck from all paralyzing experiences.

Mommy was so frail. I had never seen her like this before. And there I was, away from home, changing her, overseeing her care, ensuring that she swallowed at least a few bites of the right food as the hospital food will certainly provide you with a first-class ticket to Heaven. I was her legal healthcare provider so I was doing all I could to ensure I was working with the doctors, doing my own research, and speaking with other medical professionals about her diagnosis and appropriate next steps.

The day I gave the okay for the doctors to perform a procedure on her, which all the medical professionals agreed was best, was the day my oldest brother called the nursing station at the hospital and objected to the procedure. Although he had been calling every day to object to anything the doctors were recommending. I was living in the hospital in a chair by my mother's bedside and he was adamant and opposed everything I was telling him was best for mommy.

He challenged not just the procedure, but all things medical that were recommended for our mother. His calls, supported by my other brother and sister, became a routine. Where was this sudden, unauthorized, and counterproductive intervention coming from?

Before Mommy got sick, my siblings' presence in her life was seldom and brief. During COVID, she felt isolated and often asked me, "What did I do that they don't call often?"

I had contacted my siblings earlier during that year to ask them why they had not been more in touch with mom. It took a very long time for me to address their lack of participation, but I eventually did. After the conference call I had with my siblings to tell them mom was sad and worried about their lack of calls, they began to call mom a bit more.

The last straw, and I really mean the one that almost broke me, was their relentless push to transfer our mother from Minnesota hospital, where she lived with her husband, to Johns Hopkins in Maryland, which is where I alone live with my two girls and no support system.

Having sat in the hospital with my mom daily, I knew that she was too frail to fly from Minneapolis to Maryland. The doctors also advised me not to do so. They felt she was not strong enough and COVID was still on the rise.

I had to beg the doctors to move her to a private maternity room to prevent her and I from catching COVID. They even suggested that I go home, and that I could not just live in the hospital. I told them they would need to bring President Obama, Trump and President Biden with the entire US National Guard to get me out. I said it so respectfully and calmly that I believe they understood and saw what I was dealing with daily.

Even if I had mom transferred to John Hopkins in Maryland, upon arrival, she would be placed on a waiting list just to be admitted, and her insurance would not cover most of her costs. I also could not ever take her away from her husband, not with how close their relationship was.

When I responded to my siblings with an emphatic no to that suggestion, and explained why, I was accused of not wanting our mother in my home. This accusation cut me deeply, as I had had my parents living with me for over 25 years!

That night, my heart pounding, I wondered what I had done to my siblings. Why did they not trust my decision-making for Mom, since I had been the primary one caring for her for so many years? My home was where we gathered every year for Christmas from long before I had children until my children were in high school. I also respected my siblings, and truly love my nieces and nephews as if they were my own.

This new, defiant behavior was terribly concerning to me, especially when I had called each of my siblings at the beginning of the year, asking why they did not reach out to Mom more often. Honestly, they had received the best from my parents. They were all given property to start their adult lives, but since I was the last child, there was nothing left for me. They were put through college while I put myself through college and graduate school.

I understood that times had changed and my parents did the best they could. Where were the consultations and support when I was the sole caregiver to both of our parents? I never resented them for that, not once! I just did what I had to do, and I never asked for help.

I guess I assumed that they would join in when they could, but could not come often. I love my siblings, so I kept on doing what I could to bring the family together, but mom was aware of their absence, and her heart was broken by it.

Mom was the sweetest, kindest, and most loving person you would ever meet. She would do ANYTHING for ANYONE. She was wise and intelligent (still helping my girls with calculus homework at 82). She was a peacemaker, an influencer for the greater good, and made everyone feel like a guest of honor.

How excited we were to sit down for her meals! Her greens, potato salad, fried rice with grilled shrimp, and stringed chicken were a feast. Her soup nursed you right back to health, and her fried fish with dry rice, (if you know, you know,) warmed your bones.

She was quiet and very observant, and we'd have a whole conversation without saying a word. Our deep connection goes as far back as I can remember, and I am so grateful that it extended to my girls as well. Mom was a mother to all of us and to our friends.

Throughout my own challenges, I continued to care for Mom, and my siblings knew this. Their behavior toward me in the throes of my mom's illness was so perplexing and hurtful.

I hope you can see now why, from Mom's hospital room in Minnesota, I made the decision to place a long-overdue, full family conference call. The conversation that took place did not enlighten or soothe anyone. Because in life, it is not our title or what we have accomplished that makes us who we are. It is who we are on the inside that matters. It was then I confirmed that all the years I thought we were close was a lie. Just because people smile with you does not mean they are for you.

What a bitter pill that was to swallow from my own family. Our parents had worked so hard to make certain we were close, grounded in Christ and positioned well for our future. I was heart-broken, but could not quit as I had mom to care for while knowing my daughters were fending for themselves.

Well, sidebar over, I bring you back to the moment of my mother's illness, my feelings at her bedside.

The days with my mother in the hospital were terribly difficult. We were both adjusting to her diagnosis and her new regimen of treatment. I stayed by her bedside in a straight-backed chair and barely slept.

The rest of my life could not be put on hold because of my mother's illness. I still had to work full time while living in the hospital. I had my laptop and had to continue working while sitting by her bedside. I would go in the bathroom or find an empty room when I had to lead meetings. I had just assumed a new leadership role at work with a growing team.

There was a new manager for my division who decided, for reasons I do not know, that her agenda did not include me. Her goal was to manage me out and she was calculative in her pursuit to fulfill her plan. She was awful and threatened me every day although she knew I was in the hospital with my mom.

I should have taken leave of absence, but it is not every day a black woman finally breaks through the glass ceiling. I also thought my boss understood my challenge so I kept working. Little did I know she was damaging my reputation and trying to get me fired. I was devastated, but numb because I was dealing with my mother's illness advancing, the thoughts of death, conference call fights from my siblings, and my daughters living alone.

At the same time, my older daughter's first year of college became remote due to Covid, and she was home trying to maneuver through online classes and had to cook and drive her sister to and from school daily as I was living in the hospital with my mom in Minneapolis. My younger daughter was a senior in high school struggling to navigate the college application process.

Every day, my mother would say, you need to get back to your girls. But because of Covid, the hospital staff was very limited, so there were many days that I tended to my mother's every need. I just could not leave her bedside. The girls understood and encouraged me to remain there but to make sure I brought their grandmother home with me.

The pain of life began to cripple my zeal. I can confidently tell you that my faith in my Lord and Savior, Jesus Christ kept me from going overboard. I leaned on HIS immeasurable shoulders and took one day at a time, praying for Mom's healing. I fought to remain steadfast, but it was not easy. I was operating on fumes from so little sleep. I did my best not to lose my mind and to be an advocate for my mom, who desperately needed all the support she could get.

Through it all, the doctors were amazed as Mom continued to smile every day and took every treatment like a champ. We held hands most days until she fell asleep. I would kiss her face, and she would say, you must really love your mommy. I would say to her, as I customarily did, one thousand kisses, Mommy, and she would respond, two thousand kisses, and I would say, three thousand, until she would finally say, It's exponential, Blossom, and we would both smile.

Seeing her in constant pain and deteriorating before my eyes was the absolute worst! We continued to have hope, though, because she showed great improvement some days. She was also very aware of the challenges I was facing with family, work, and being away from home. She encouraged me to go home, as I needed a change of clothes, a good bath, and a good night's sleep, but I could not bring myself to leave her.

Needless to say, I could not go home for Thanksgiving. But isn't it home wherever the people you love are? I came up with a plan. Mom knew we'd be having a quiet Thanksgiving at the hospital with my stepdad (Mr. B.), and Harriette, his daughter, who loved my mom dearly, as did all his children.

On Thanksgiving morning, I told Mom that I had a surprise for her. She remained quiet in the chair next to the bed, looking out the window at the lake below. At around 11 am, I said, "Mom, look who's here. She slowly turned and saw my daughters, Mia Blossom and Jaden Christina, walk into the room. Light seemed to beam from her face as she tried to leap out of her chair!

She screamed, Oh, my God! My daughters hugged their grandma so tight. It was a hug that appeared to last forever. Tears slowly rolled down our faces, and for me, that moment froze in time. Looking back now, I understand why.

Then Mom turned to me and exclaimed, Blossom, you have given me more than a million bucks! She turned back to the girls and wrapped her arms around them again. We all had a wonderful time in the Jones Harrison rehabilitation facility.

I eventually went home for Christmas, as Mommy continued to show signs of improvement. On the first day back to work after the Christmas holidays, I got the worst phone call of my life. The doctors told me Mom had taken a turn for the worse, and there was nothing they could do.

I flew out on the first flight I could find, and when I got to my mom in the hospital, she smiled and said, You're back again? I said, Yep, Mommy and I'm not going anywhere. She smiled and said, "It's okay. I'm fine. I just want to go home."

I took her home and remained by her bedside, holding her hand, feeding her, and making sure she had her moisturizer and that her hair was done daily. My step-dad and his daughter and her husband were there also caring for her. My brothers and sister did come to see our mom briefly as they had to return to work.

A week and a half later, my mother passed away, holding my hand while I kissed her face and told her I love you. She waved goodbye to me and told me, smiling, "It's okay, I'm going to see Jesus now." It was a gut-wrenching yet beautiful transition. Many family members, including all of her children and stepchildren, got there in time to say goodbye, and she passed away smiling as I told her for the last time, I love you mommy, and I faintly saw her try to respond, "I love you Blossom," That meant the world, to say the least.

My mother entered Heaven with one thousand kisses, and I can still feel her hands laced in mine. My mother was my everything.

My mother entered Heaven with one thousand kisses, and I can still feel her hands laced in mine. My mother was my everything.

She was the family the girls and I knew.

She had two funerals, as the family in Minnesota said they could not let her go back to Maryland without honoring her. Both funerals were very well-attended, and everyone who spoke said that they had never met a woman like her. People came from all over to pay their respects. Although there were many dignitaries in attendance, I was humbled by the workers from the Baldacci grocery store, a lady from the post office, dollar store, and dry cleaners who all remembered my mom.

My stepdad, although devastated, was strong enough to sit with his hand on her casket. He stood and spoke so lovingly of her. All her grandchildren spoke so fondly of her and were in tears. When my girls spoke of their grandma, they brought the audience to tears and made me so proud. The entire church was in tears. I realized then that Mommy would always be with me, as I could see her imprint on my girls.

As days passed, and my mother's absence was my new reality, I was more than stuck; I was frozen. Losing my mother and being there for my girls, who were obviously broken, was terribly difficult. They were so accustomed to having Grandma in their lives. Even when she was away, we would talk to her every morning before work and school and every evening at dinner.

It was very hard to adjust to life without her. Two weeks after burying my mother, my oldest brother, Clarence, who lived overseas, suddenly passed away. I had just spoken to him two weeks before.

What do you do when life turns left and veers completely out of control? How do you continue to move forward and make progress when life as you know it changes for the worse?

I had no more emotion. I was not cold, but callused, and I knew I had to take my own advice from this book and get help.

The story I just told you in this 3rd chapter, Don't Quit, happened while I was writing this book. And I had to share it to show you that even on the very brink of quitting, which is where I was, you can still find the strength to come back. Understand that the challenges in life, though devastating, prepares you for the life you are designed to live.

Earlier in the book, I told you a little bit about my life as a 16 -year-old graduating from high school and starting college. Let me elaborate so you can see where the early seeds of Don't Quit were planted for me.

I told you that my parents, through no fault of their own, lost everything. You see, I was raised in Monrovia, the capital city of Liberia in Western Africa. We lived in a middle-class neighborhood, and our house was filled with love.

Sensing the political unrest that was about to come, my parents sent me to the States to live with my cousin. I had just finished high school! Well, my parents' sense of the unrest came true. They were forced to leave their home, leaving absolutely everything behind. They had to walk 45 miles through untraveled terrain just to make it to safety. Right after that, all communication was cut off, and I didn't hear from them for three years.

I'm sure you can imagine how devastating this was for me. To make it worse, I was about to register for my second semester of college, and the tuition was supposed to be coming from my parents. I had no clue where I would get the first dime to pay for school. I knew that working part-time for $8 per hour, which I had negotiated up from $5 would not come close to my tuition at Howard University.

I felt lost and broken because I could not contact the only people who I knew truly loved me. I did not know if they were alive or dead. But I knew my education was a way for me to get a better-paying job.

Early one morning, on registration day for school, I stood in line, terrified. I was about to sign up for classes, knowing that I had no money to pay for tuition. I also had to make sure that I signed up only for classes that were scheduled early in the morning, as I had to work two jobs; one in the afternoon immediately after my last class and one starting in the evening and going until late at night.

After waiting in line for hours, I finally made it to the front of the line. I slowly walked to the registrar's window. I provided her with the list of classes that I needed to take, and she said, "OK, give me a few minutes." Then she said those words that haunted my soul, "How do you intend to pay?"

That which you pursue relentlessly will produce the outcome you desire.

I had rehearsed in my mind how I was going to tell her my situation, that as soon as I heard from my parents, they would send me the money for school. Keep in mind, I was barely 17 and terrified, but somehow, the following words came out of my mouth with confidence: "Oh, my father owns this school, and he will cover everything I need."

We looked at each other for a moment, and then she said, "Oh, I'm sorry I did not know," and registered me for all my classes. I was speaking, of course, of my Heavenly Father, but she thought something else. I was ecstatic!

I knew that soon I would hear from my parents, and before the semester was over, my tuition would be paid. Or so I thought. I did not hear back from my parents for three long years, so I had to drop out of school. I continued working two jobs in order to chase my dreams. It was not easy, and I wanted to quit so many times as I felt life was going nowhere. I hated working for people who were not kind and who saw me as less. But I knew that if I quit, life would get even harder, so I had to keep pressing forward.

I eventually did go back to school and kept working toward my goal. I now have one undergraduate degree in Computer Science and two master's degrees in Software Engineering and a Global MBA from Georgetown University and an executive degree in Cybersecurity and Policy from Harvard University.

I mentioned these universities only to show you that anything is possible if you focus, you can work anywhere you choose in this world! The sweetest part of my story is that my parents did make it to the US and spent over 25 years living with me! Don't fear the Pain – it is what prepares you!

Don't fear the Pain – it is what prepares you!

I hope that the stories from my recent and distant past will empower you. Whatever you do, when life spins even more out of control than you can imagine, do NOT quit.

There were so many times I felt like quitting, but I knew I had to keep pushing. It is not easy to go after what you really want, but the truth is that nothing worth having will be acquired easily. This is intentional so you can value the loads of wealth that will come and empower others.

Now, will you arrive where you want to be overnight? No, you will not. Will life turn out exactly the way you plan every single time? No, but let me ask you this: Would you rather remain stuck? Would you rather live without some plan for the life you want? Do you want life to just happen to you, or do you want to make your life happen?

You are reading this book because you do not want life to just happen to you. Yes, it takes a lot of work to achieve your goals, but it also takes work to remain stagnant. Remaining stagnant takes a toll on your mind and body. It is time for you to decide where you will put your efforts.

Will your path always be clear? Absolutely not. If it is, you are on someone else's path. Even though you do not have all the answers or resources and cannot see your path clearly, you must be purposeful about the life you want to live.

Keep taking small steps daily. When you get tired, take a break, but please keep making little progress. Your dreams will most definitely come to pass if you keep looking ahead and making progress.

Please understand no one is going to make it all come together for you. If they do, then they own you. You must fight for what you want. Some days will seem easy, but others, so difficult. Don't forget: The difficulties are there for your good. The process is strengthening you for your purpose, your why.

The five steps in this book will definitely help you move forward and help you live the life you want. They have worked for me and many others. I still review these five steps for every phase of my life to make certain I am sticking to my plan because I know the outcome they produce.

When the going gets tough, and you get tired, disappointed, frustrated, just do not quit! Don't quit on YOU!

As a reminder, here are the five steps:

1. Get Rid of Negative Beliefs.
2. Decide Who You Want to Become.
3. Take Action and be Relentless.
4. Get Help! Please!
5. Prepare for Success.

Let me say this to you: That which you pursue relentlessly will produce the outcome you are looking for. As a matter of fact, the pain and challenges you will face along the way will pale compared to the rewards you will see, so stay the course.

The pain and the challenges help you define your path more clearly. Even if you stumble, you will learn. Don't quit.

Setbacks teach you something that cannot be taught in a classroom.

They build your muscle to learn, and they prepare you for the next turn in your life. So, change your perspective about failure. . Either you will win, or you will learn; either way, you gain so stay on track.

I can understand how, at about this point in the book, you might be thinking, "Oh, sure, Blossom, follow the five steps in this book. That's easy for you to say!" No, no, it is not easy for me to say at all. These five steps did not appear magically on the page as I sat down to write. Each step showed itself to me, slowly and singularly, as I agonized over digging as deep down into myself as I possibly could to become unstuck from places of darkness, many of which I have shared with you.

- Step 1: Get rid of negative beliefs? No, not easy to say or do. I needed clarity. My thoughts were clogged. Because paralysis took over, I could not determine what to do next. My responsibilities were so consuming I couldn't imagine how to unravel them to visualize my big dreams.

- Step 2: Decide what you want to become. Not easy at all. I would ask myself, "Blossom, who do you want to be?" Every day, many times a day, I wanted to become the person who protects herself from events and emotions just to feel safe.

- Step 3: Take action and be relentless. This one was particularly tough. This book is about becoming unstuck. I was so stuck that I felt like I would be stuck within stuck forever.

- Step 4: Get help! Please! It took time, so much time, to be ok with reaching out, with letting people know that I was hurting, with exposing my vulnerability.

- Step 5: Prepare for Success. I would have scoffed at them if those words had even entered my thoughts early on! Success? What is that?

Trust me on this: It is through wading through adversity, clawing through false starts, missteps, wrong turns, and spiraling doubt that these steps showed themselves to me, one by one, slowly empowering me to help myself and get unstuck.

Will you sometimes get tired of trying? Yes. Will challenges appear insurmountable? Absolutely. Stay focused anyway. No matter what comes your way, don't quit. Also, be wise about who you spend time with. They are either adding to you or taking away from you.

The advantage of staying focused is slowly forming a habit of making progress by taking little baby steps. Soon, what seemed so very difficult in the beginning will be easier for you. Follow the five steps listed in this book, and they will definitely help you to live the life you want now.

Chapter 4

Make Adjustments

What You Believe Will Happen WILL Actually Happen.

When life takes an unexpected turn, and it will say, "This is happening for my good." Keep saying it until you are convinced. As I have said repeatedly, know who you want to become and understand your "why." Even if you don't have all the answers, keep speaking what you want and take small steps toward your success.

When necessary, please get some help. Talk to someone you respect and trust, or engage a professional. You are not an island. Know the temptations that distract you, rob you, and steal your time. Whatever you feed will grow, so kill the monster in you while it is little.

I learned this exercise from a life coach:

Look yourself in the mirror and say seven things you are proud of, then say seven things for which you need to forgive yourself, and last, state seven things you will commit to doing. Repeat each of these daily, looking at yourself in a mirror. Over time, you will be surprised at how free and empowered you are becoming.

Making adjustments will help you derive the precision you need to carve out and display what you are trying to accomplish. Sometimes, the adjustments you will need to make are minor. They require small tweaks rather than major surgery. It could be the small areas in your life that you need to evaluate.

Here are a few examples I learned to make adjustments to my progress. In the evening, do the following:

1. Take a few minutes to evaluate your day and score yourself on how you performed in different areas. Pay attention to the low grades because they inform you. When you score consistently high in an aspect of your day, you know it is an aspect that comes easily or one that you have mastered. Do this consistently, and you will begin to see a pattern of where your weaknesses lie and what you need to change. This assessment will inform you on

where you might seek advice on how to make these adjustments.

2. Write down what you need to do the next day and make it time bound. Set a deadline for when you need to be done.

3. Incorporate exercise, eliminate junk food, and drink plenty of water throughout your day. Even if it is just fifteen or twenty minutes, do some exercise daily. Try not to eat your heaviest meal in the evening.

4. Unplug from your devices. I am also continuously making progress here as I work with people in different time zones. But do all you can to disconnect at some point before you go to bed. At least thirty minutes before bedtime.

5. Connect with your loved ones. No one is an island, and two are always better than one. If you live alone, hopefully, you will have some healthy friendships and people who care for you. For well over 25 years, I took care of my parents. In the early years, it was while I was raising two small children. Later, as a single mom, I began building my career. The truth is, I had no time to form and nurture friendships as my life as a caregiver for my

parents and children took most of my free time. Does this sound familiar to you? If it does, please stay focused on your goal and your "why" anyway. Life is full of pleasant surprises.

6. Spend some time reading. If I may suggest, read about people who have already accomplished what you are trying to do or simply stay informed about your area of expertise. Learn something new! You can also read a book that empowers you or takes you on a much-needed mental vacation.

7. Write down what you are grateful for and capture how you want your next day to be.

8. Prepare what you need to make your morning easier. It may be picking out an outfit for the next day (Thank God we were not quarantined forever), preparing your lunch, or setting up your morning routine. It's always easier to be organized in the morning.

9. Have a few minutes of quiet time just relaxing or in prayer and meditation.

10. Get to bed earlier than you anticipated. It is terribly critical for you to rest well. When I do, I can conquer the world! It is also good for your health, as we live in such a fast- paced world.

When the going gets tough and you get tired and frustrated, just do not quit! Don't quit on YOU!

Try to continuously assess these areas:

- Your spiritual life – How is it? If it is not where it should be, work on it. If you place first things first, everything else will fall into place. Remember, your spirit provides you with discernment and wisdom. Without discernment and wisdom, how successful can you be? Read your Bible so you can understand for yourself, (not what you heard, and not what you were told,) how amazingly loving and Oh what a way-maker Jesus is!
- Your goals or your mission – Are you clear about what you want to do and who you want to become? Can you say it in one sentence? I have a mission statement. You should develop one too, and commit it to memory.
- Family – Family is everything. Do you have a healthy relationship with your family? Does your family give you good energy? Have you forgiven whoever hurt you? Stop right here if there are some unresolved issues. Do your very best to forgive them or forgive yourself. You

don't want unresolved issues walking with you into your future. They will be more expensive to fix later. They are baggage that you do not need to bear.

- Friends – Who is in your immediate circle? Is it adding to you or taking away from you? You should connect with people who are like-minded, who are going where you want to go, or at least are successful in their own lane. You don't want to be around people who drain your energy or cause you to behave in a way you may regret.

- Finances – Are you living below your means? Are you saving? Are you investing? Get an advisor who is a fiduciary. Do you have an emergency fund established? Are you responsible with your spending habits? Do you have high-interest credit cards or loans? Develop a plan to eliminate debt and be aggressive about it. Get rid of depreciating assets. Live on a budget. Discipline with money is essential. You don't want to lose everything you've worked so very hard for.

- Mental Health – How are you doing in this area? Even if you believe you are good, can you please seek professional help just to assess where you are? Engaging with a therapist is like getting a tune-up. Our cars need it, and so do we!

- Growing – Are you learning something new? Are you seeking awareness about your industry, your community, and the world? It is critical to stay relevant and influence the future in which you and the next generation will be living.

- Giving - Think hard about this. Make sure it is a heart action when you give, not an action for which you seek recognition. Remember, to whom much is given, much will be required. And what you receive from giving is always greater than what you give.

- Succession planning - Think beyond yourself. Will your plan be beneficial to those you leave behind? Think of your future. Do you have a will and Trust? Life insurance? If you own a business, who will run it in your absence? What you are building must be greater than you, or you are on a ride that has an ending.

Lastly, life will have its challenges for sure, but there is nothing that you will face that can totally limit you if your mind's made up. What you believe will happen

WILL TRULY HAPPEN. Change what you believe about yourself, say what you want to see happen in your life, write it down, and take the necessary steps!

I can't emphasize enough: The five steps in this book will definitely help you live the life you want. Here are the five steps again:

1. Get Rid of Negative Beliefs.
2. Decide Who You Want to Become.
3. Take Action and be Relentless.
4. Get Help! Please!
5. Prepare for Success.

It has worked for people I have coached and people who have heard me speak. It has worked for me! I have developed a journal that goes along with this book to help you capture your goals and associated actions for each area. Your vision comes to life when you write it down, so be diligent in documenting it. It will benefit you much more than you know.

You have more inside of you than you realize!

I graduated from high school at the age of 16 and I thought I would have been done with college by age 20 and completed my masters by the age of 23. As I mentioned previously, none of what I thought happened as expected and I had to make life for myself right after high school. Being separated from my parents and family was the absolute worst! I had no means of income and all my plans to go to college went out the window as I had to find work to feed myself and find a place to lay my head. I was broken, lost, and stuck! I had plenty of reasons to give up, but thank God I did not.

I kept saying to myself there has to be a better way and I have to fight for me and the future my parents worked so hard to give their children. For many years I struggled and faced many challenges, but a mind that is consistently fixed on pushing towards a better life will always succeed.

A mind that is consistently fixed on pushing towards a better life will always succeed.

You must understand this will only happen if you are willing to make the sacrifice that progress requires as I alluded to earlier.

Working two jobs and going to school was not easy, but by God's Grace I persevered. Today, I not only have an undergraduate in Computer Science, but two masters. One in Software Engineering and the other a global MBA from Georgetown University. I also completed an executive degree from Harvard University on the Intersection of Cybersecurity and Policy.

In my early career, after college, I worked for Lockheed Martin as a Software Engineer, and moved on after many years and eventually became the Cybersecurity Advisor to the CIO of a major three letter agency. Today, I am Director of Cybersecurity and AI at one of the top cybersecurity companies in the world.

I consistently follow these five steps to become unstuck and it has landed me to where I am today. I had to get rid of negative beliefs - I was believing that someone was coming to rescue me from the hard life or there was no way I was going to make it. I had to change that belief and say to myself everyday you can do whatever you put your mind to.

Then I had to decide who I wanted to become. I knew I wanted to be an engineer so I began taking the steps daily to research where and how I could affordably enroll in school to continue my education. There were times I could only afford to take two classes at a time, but I was relentless as I did not like working odd jobs and being treated like dirt.

Did everything work out perfectly? Absolutely not. Life happened and the challenges continued, but because of the consistent pursuit and a made-up mind I had unknowingly built a resilience that allowed me to face life's challenges knowing that if I could get through the previous challenge, I could certainly get through another.

I eventually was able to get some help and continue to renew my mind daily with the Word of God. I also promised that I would let no one steal my joy and rob me of the Blossom GOD intended for me to be.

Remember this quote I read a long time ago: "Never regret being a good person to the wrong people. Your behavior says everything about you, and their behavior says everything about them."

Today I continue to prepare for success. As the Director for Cybersecurity and AI, I still follow these steps and have taught my children and many others. As you may know, the advancement in Cybersecurity and AI has progressed leaps and bounds and will continue to do so. In my role I have to continuously learn and get certified in certain areas every year to remain relevant and influence the direction of Artificial Intelligence and Cybersecurity.

I also continue working in my lab, simulating challenges and working towards a resolve. As a leader, I want to not only influence the business strategically, but be relevant tactically on how we achieve our objectives and key results. I still write down a plan for the top three things I need to do to "Win my Week" and I do so both professionally and personally.

I also write down my plan to continue to be successful for the year and the years to come, and I take small steps daily and get help as required. This all came together simply by getting rid of negative belief and believing that I can be whoever I want to be.

Understand this, the effort that you put in today, although it may be challenging and even boring at times, but it will most definitely cause you to live unstuck and bring you the success you are after. Continue to follow these five steps. The benefits they will bring you will far exceed the work you put in.

Step into your life of continued success today! You have way more inside of you than you realize. I know you can make it happen. If I can make it, so can you! Remember, the vision in your mind must be bigger than the fear in your heart.

In the words of my wise and beautiful mother, "Your table is set. Now go and eat!"

Live the life you want, now!

Chapter 4

Chapter 4

About the Author

Blossom has an innate passion to see others succeed. She is a technical leader in Artificial Intelligence and Cybersecurity and has been in the field for over fifteen years. She speaks at conferences, universities, and organizations, both  domestically and internationally. She has spoken to many universities about roles in STEM and to organizations on exceeding expected results.

She has an undergraduate in Computer Science and a master in Software Engineering from the University of Maryland. She also holds a Masters from Georgetown University on Global Leadership and an Executive Degree from Harvard University.

With all her accomplishments, she has an undeniable

passion to empower others to succeed. She is a Professional Speaker, Life Strategist and Author.

She has positively impacted the lives of many domestically and internationally. Her life story is powerful and gripping, and her message is one everyone must hear. She is a woman on a mission to empower organizations and people to achieve their desired results.

www.blossombaker.com

Email: info@blossombaker.com

instagram: blossombakerspeaks